I CAN COOK

HAITIAN FUSION RECIPES INSPIRED BY
A FIRST GENERATION'S CULINARY VOYAGE

AYIDA SOLÉ
OF THE HAITIAN CROISSANT

Copyright © 2023 by The Haitian Croissant LLC
Food Photographs copyright © 2022 by Britt Belo
Food Photographs copyright ©2023 by Myesha Evon
Atomospheric photographs ©2022-2023 by Myesha Evon
Haiti Atomospheric photographs pg 10-17,47,60,78 ©2022-2023 by Jean Oscar A
Cover illustration copyright © 2023 by Syrine Ben Slimane
Additional Credits on page 90

All rights reserved. No portion of this book may be reproduced- mechanically, electronically or by and other means, including photocopying- without written permission of the publisher.

Library of Congress Cataloging in Publication Data is on file.
ISBN 979-8-218-33142-9

Art Direction and Design by Ayida Solé Consulting

For speaking engagements,
contact: thehaitiancroissant@gmail.com
@thehaitiancroissant
Youtube: Ayida Solé

To my mom.

To Tandan.
To my tribe.
To my fellow first-gen croissants striving to make their families proud.

To Ayiti, for making me who I am and constantly inspiring me to create.

TABLE OF CONTENTS

I. ABOUT

II. AUTHOR'S NOTE

III. INTRODUCTION

IV. YON TI PLEZI

V. BUILDING FLAVOR

VI. QUICK-FAST

VII. PLANTAIN SUPREMACY

VIII. FOR A CROWD

IX. FOR THE SOUL

X. YOU CAN COOK

ABOUT THE AUTHOR

Ayida "The Haitian Croissant" Solé is a Haitian-American designer, home cook, creative consultant, and gastro-visionary. She is also the Founder and Director of The Haitian Croissant Foundation.

Ayida Solé earned her nickname, "The Haitian Croissant," while living abroad in Paris, France. In 2020, during the worldwide COVID-19 pandemic, she launched the online brand to connect with the Haitian community in Paris. Today, The Haitian Croissant is a brand that celebrates Haitian culture through original recipes, travel, design, and culinary experiences. The platform invites people to explore and immerse themselves in the Haitian diaspora. Ayida Solé serves as an unofficial ambassador of Haiti, working to elevate Haitian culture in the global media.

Furthermore, Ayida Solé is a creative director and brand consultant for emerging businesses, personalities, and luxury brands. She possesses a formal educational background in both the fashion and culinary industries.

AUTHOR'S NOTE

As a Haitian American, I've been fortunate to be surrounded by great cooks throughout my life. My cooking style is a blend of three influential women: my mother, an independent woman straight outta Okap who always prioritizes health; my godmother, Tante Dan, an exceptional non-professionally trained cook who, in my opinion, is the best; and my grandmother, who created simple meals that always tasted like love. Each of these remarkable women imparted recipes that I've continued to use and adapt over the years. My grandmother's pasta, my mother's rice and beans, and Tante Dan's lasagna are dishes that I know will never disappoint me or a crowd. The first meal I learned to cook was spaghetti and tomato sauce when I was just seven years old.

During my childhood, I spent Saturday mornings with my godmother. The Food Network was always on, and I eagerly watched alongside her as she cooked. Emeril Lagasse's enthusiastic "BAM" filled me with excitement, and Ina Garten taught me how to host, sparking dreams of one day hosting my own dinner parties as a grown-up. The combination of these shows and my godmother's cooking and baking created a constant sensory euphoria in me. As far back as I can remember, different dishes and flavors have transported me to key moments in my past.

I moved out of my mother's apartment at the age of 17, gaining the freedom to experiment in the kitchen. However, it wasn't until I moved out of state for college and into my own apartment that I truly began to explore cooking techniques and develop various culinary hacks, particularly in Haitian cuisine.

Leaving home and living on your own often provides ample opportunities to discover who you are, your true likes and dislikes. Learning to cook for yourself helps you uncover these complexities. I've discovered that my food must always possess intricate flavors and textures, yet I also value convenience. The theme of "The I Can Cook Book" is centered on flavor and convenience. My aim is to empower you with the confidence to whip up a meal for yourself or for a guest who declares their hunger. The satisfaction that emanates from a delicious meal you've prepared will inspire you to experiment with the next culinary adventure.

While I've mainly mentioned spaghetti and lasagna thus far, this book will equip you with the tools to cook both traditional and fusion Haitian dishes in a reasonable amount of time. With my help, you will proudly be able to say "I Can Cook," to your family and friends.

Blessings and more,
Ayida "The Haitian Croissant" Solé

INTRODUCTION

In a world of instant gratification and quick pleasures, one of the coolest things to be able to say is, "I can cook." Growing up in a Haitian household ensured that I was never short of flavorful dishes to enjoy. For those of us with working parents, Sunday meals were highly anticipated because they meant a new dish to savor throughout the week. My single mother, like many others in her position, would prepare enough food to last at least the first half of the week, ensuring everyone was well-fed. While I was grateful for the nourishment, my love for luxury cuisine began at a young age—blame it on The Food Network.

To me, the luxury was being able to eat something new every day, mirroring the chefs I admired on television. This revelation prompted me to learn how to cook, desiring variety beyond what my loving mother had prepared just two days prior. I vividly recall the first time I stepped into the kitchen at the age of 7, declaring to my mom that I would handle dinner. I recreated a dish my grandmother always made for me upon her return from her 6-month stint in Haiti—spaghetti. My version was a simple spaghetti with tomato sauce and an excessive amount of cloves ("jirof" in Kreyol). I was, and still am, obsessed with the taste of cloves. It took me a few years to realize that not everyone shares my enthusiasm for cloves and that I shouldn't drown my dishes in them.

Many of my childhood memories are intertwined with music and food, making eating an immersive experience for me. The Haitian dishes I adore are directly linked to specific moments during my yearly trips to Haiti. Whether it's the love of patat ak let (sweet potato and milk), discovered in St Michel, a countryside in Haiti, or the appreciation for mayi moulin ak fey (polenta and spinach), developed at my uncle's best friend's house in Petion Ville, each dish has a story. Now, with The Haitian Croissant Foundation, I annually invite friends from diverse backgrounds to Haiti to experience the country through service and savor dishes unavailable in the States—flavors and ingredients have a heightened freshness in Haiti. My love for Haiti is reflected in the fusion dishes I create, drawing inspiration from my global travels while staying true to the traditional recipes forming the backbone of Haitian cooking.

"I Can Cook" is divided into five chapters: Building Flavors, Quick Fast, Plantain Supremacy, For a Crowd, and For the Soul. Each chapter delves into the layers defining Haitian cuisine from my perspective. Haitian cuisine stands out due to its unique flavors and fresh ingredients and traditionally, we do not measure ingredients, we let our ancestors guide us in the kitchen. I on the other hand have provided meausurements for you to get familiar with the ingredients, but as you repeat these recipes and get familiar, you will also learn to ignore measurements and trust your spirit. As I continue on a wellness journey, and share what I have learned, I've removed addictive ingredients like Maggi, replacing them with fresh ground spices. Fried foods are minimized, and every recipe includes a plant-based alternative because Haitian food is meant to be enjoyed by everyone. My hope is that through the recipes shared in this book, readers will glimpse the nuances shaping Haitian cuisine through a refined yet effective lens.

YON TI PLEZI

In a Haitian household, good music and food go hand in hand. A great song is always there to complement your meal. Cooking becomes ten times more enjoyable when you can vibe out and dance. In Haitian Kreyol, we call simple pleasures " Yon ti plezi," It is only right that I provide you with the simple pleasure of a playlist to cook the following recipes to.

Scan the QR code below to access the official "I Can Cook" playlist, enjoy the sweet imagery of Haiti and let's get cooking!

CHAPTER I
BUILDING FLAVOR

BUILDING FLAVORS

Becoming a comfortable, intuitive cook is all about trusting your taste. If you've never been savvy in the kitchen, it can be hard to rely on your culinary senses initially. Ensuring you have the necessary ingredients for a successful dish is essential, and when you run out of certain items, resourcefully use what you have.

After years of experiential home cooking, I've curated a list of spices and cooking staples that I always keep on hand to enhance the flavors of my meals. As you continue to cook, learn to maintain a running list of spices that are running low in your spice cabinet and restock them before you run out completely. This way, you'll always be well-stocked with the essentials. In my fridge, there's always a mason jar filled with Essential Epis and Pink Pikliz, Haitian staples for building flavor profiles.

In my pantry at all times, I I consistently stock the following to help me build on flavors and whip out a recipe in a jiffy:

A CLUTCH PANTRY

Spices
- Salt
- Pepper
- Cayenne Pepper
- Paprika
- Red Pepper Flakes
- Turmeric
- Cumin
- Curry Powder
- Oregano
- Onion Powder
- Garlic Powder
- Cinnamon
- Cloves
- White Vinegar
- Everything but the Bagel Seasoning

Misc
- Coconut or Brown Sugar
- Avocado Oil
- Olive Oil
- Cornstarch
- Baking Powder
- Baking Soda
- Vinegar
- Soy Sauce
- BBQ Sauce
- Tomato Sauce
- Canned Coconut Milk
- Red Kidney Beans
- Jasmine Rice

Cleaning
- Bar Keepers Friend
- Steel Wool

ESSENTIAL EPIS

Epis plays a pivotal role in Haitian cooking and cuisine. Essentially, it's a blended mixture of fresh herbs and spices used for marinating seafood, poultry, meats, and vegetables. In Haitian Kreyol, "epis" serves as both a noun and an adjective. As a cook, you never want to hear that your food is missing "epis," which would imply that you skimped on seasoning and, consequently, lacked flavor. I'm here to ensure that your kitchen never lacks flavor. Make a commitment to whip up a fresh batch of my Essential Epis once a month, and you can store it in your fridge for up to three weeks.

Serving Time: 10min

Serving Size: 10

Ingredients:

- **1 bush of scallion**
- **1 bunch of Parsley**
- **1 Green Bell Pepper, sliced and seeded**
- **Juice of 1 Lime**
- **1 Habanero Pepper**
- **1 Red Bell Pepper, sliced and seeded**
- **1 Medium Red Onion**
- **7 Cloves of Garlic**
- **1 Yellow Bell Pepper, sliced and seeded**
- **1 teaspoon Salt**
- **1/2 cup White Distilled Vinegar**

Instructions:

1. Begin by slicing the bell peppers and removing the seeds.
2. In a blender, combine all the ingredients and blend until you achieve a smooth texture.
3. Store the mixture in an airtight jar or mason jar for future use.
4. Enjoy your versatile Epis, ready to enhance the flavor of your dishes!
5. For exceptionally tender meat and poultry, marinate in Essential Epis over night for maximum flavors

TIP *Portion two tablespoons of Essential Epis into an ice cube tray, freeze overnight, and store the cubes in a large freezer ziplock bag. This way, you'll have quick access to your Essential Epis throughout the month.*

PINK PIKLIZ

Pikliz is perhaps the simplest yet most delicious addition to any Haitian dish, and unquestionably a must-have when you're delving into the world of Haitian cuisine. Its strength lies in its very name – "pickled." Pikliz is a blend of cabbage, onion, carrots, habanero pepper, select spices, and white vinegar. Traditionally, white cabbage is used in making pikliz, but personally, I adore the rich, deep fuchsia hue that purple cabbage imparts, so that's my preferred choice when crafting it. Pikliz can elevate the flavors of dishes like rice, plantains, various meats, and more.

Serving Time: 15min   **Serving Size: 4**

Ingredients:

- 1 cup White Cabbage
- ½ cup Purple Cabbage
- 1 cup Shredded Carrot
- ½ Medium Red Onion
- 1 tablespoon Salt
- ½ teaspoon Ground Clove
- 1 tablespoon All-Purpose Seasoning
- 1 ½ cups White Distilled Vinegar
- Juice of 1 Lime
- 3 Scotch Bonnet Peppers
- Juice of half a Sour Orange

Instructions:

1. Start by cleaning and patting dry all your fruits and vegetables.
2. Using a cheese grater or potato peeler, shred the cabbage and carrots. Thinly slice the onion and scotch bonnet.
3. In a medium mixing bowl, place the shredded cabbage, carrots, onion, salt, ground clove, and Scotch Bonnet peppers
4. Pour the white distilled vinegar and sour orange juice over the vegetable mixture.
5. Mix everything together thoroughly using a pair of tongs.
6. Refrigerate the mixture and serve when ready or transfer it into a medium-sized mason jar for storage.
7. The longer your Pink Pikliz sits in its juices, the more intensely the flavors will infuse – I recommend preparing your Pink Pikliz at least 4 hours in advance before serving it.

TIP: *There is one essential rule when it comes to Pink Pikliz: Never double-dip with a used utensil; doing so will immediately compromise your batch of Pink Pikliz.*

BUSSIN' BUTTER

One of the beautiful aspects of traveling to different countries is the opportunity to embrace elements of other cultures' cuisines and incorporate them into your own. This approach is the essence of fusion cooking. Living in France, I've developed an appreciation for butter that I never had growing up. With the myriad of delicious butter flavors available, I couldn't resist joining in the excitement. Bussin' Butter lives up to its name – it's phenomenally delicious. The base of this butter is Essential Epis, so these two recipes complement each other perfectly. Elevate your sandwiches or coat your poultry with Bussin Butter, and you'll be pleasantly surprised by the results.

BUSSIN BUTTER

While Bussin' Butter may not be a traditional staple in Haitian cooking, it's certainly an essential in my kitchen! I use it on toast, marinating proteins, anything you can imagine- it goes!

Serving Time: 20min

Serving Size: 10

Ingredients:

- 8 oz High-quality salted Butter, at room temperature (Kerrygold and Beurre D'isigny are my preferred choices; Dairy-Free butter can be used as a substitute)
- 2 tbsp Essential Epis
- ½ tbsp Paprika
- ½ tbsp Oregano
- ½ tbsp Pepper
- ½ tsp Salt
- ½ tbsp Garlic Powder
- 2 tbsp Chopped Parsley

Instructions:

1. In a medium mixing bowl, whisk the room temperature butter until it becomes smooth.
2. Add in the Essential Epis, paprika, oregano, salt, pepper, garlic powder, and chopped parsley.
3. Blend the mixture with a spatula until all the ingredients are thoroughly incorporated.
4. You can either store the herb butter in a butter tin or shape it into a butter stick by rolling it on a large sheet of parchment paper.
5. Refrigerate the herb butter until it becomes solid.
6. Enjoy your delicious Bussin' Butter, perfect for enhancing the flavor of various dishes!

TIP — *This Bussin' Butter will take any sandwich, toast or protein to the next level. Marinate your proteins in this butter over night for maximum flavor.*

CHAPTER II

QUICK FAST

QUICK FAST

There's a reason they say breakfast is the most important meal of the day. While you're asleep, your body spends hours rejuvenating, and the first foods you consume upon waking set the tone for the day. Traditionally, Haitian breakfasts are quite hearty, intended to sustain you until a late lunch or early dinner. However, these dishes often require a significant amount of time to prepare, and in a fast-paced country, there isn't always enough time for such recipes on a daily basis. Consequently, I've embraced lighter options as my go-to breakfast choices. I alternate between a hearty fruit smoothie and "Pain ak Zaboka" – Avocado Toast. Embracing a mainly plant-based diet allows me to experiment with various toppings to keep things interesting.

THE "GO TO"

This smoothie recipe evokes the ones my mom used to make for me as a child. Back then, I wasn't necessarily fond of dark leafy greens, but I understood their nutritional value. Once I moved out on my own, I found myself craving this smoothie and steering clear of traditional heavy American breakfasts that often leave you feeling sluggish. Healthy habits are instilled early on, and it's up to you to incorporate them into your daily life as you gain independence in the kitchen. The inclusion of dark leafy greens in this mix is an ideal way to start your day – a perfect balance of fruit and veggies.

Serving Time: 10 min

Serving Size: 1

Ingredients:

- **1 peeled Banana**
- **1 cup of Blueberries**
- **1 cup frozen Raspberries**
- **½ cup Almond Milk (or any dairy free alternative)**
- **1 cup Spinach**
- **1 tbsp Hemp Seeds**
- **1/2 cup Ice**

Instructions:

1. Start by washing and patting dry the blueberries, spinach, and raspberries.
2. In a blender, combine all the ingredients.
3. Blend the mixture until it reaches a smooth consistency.
4. Enjoy it as a refreshing smoothie or use it as the base for a delicious smoothie bowl.
5. Savor the refreshing goodness of The Go-To!

Switch out the fruits for seasonal varieties throughout the year to tantalize your taste buds. Feel free to add your choice of protein powder when returning from a strenuous workout!

SMOOTH PAPAYE

Fresh fruit juices, known as "Jus Naturel," are a daily staple in Haiti. Popular flavors include lime, passion fruit, and Caribbean cherry. These juices are typically hand-prepared using just three simple ingredients: the fruit, water, and sugar, resulting in a fresh and revitalizing beverage. However, hand-pressed juices take more time than a classic smoothie. That's why I adore a Haitian papaya smoothie. This smoothie is so delightful that it could easily pass for dessert, but it's an excellent choice for a morning energy boost. The lime and vanilla perfectly complement the papaya, eliminating the occasional bitter aftertaste.

Serving Time: 10-15min

Ingredients:

- 1 cup Frozen Papaya
- 1 cup Almond Milk or Dairy-Free Alternative
- ¼ cup Canned Coconut Milk
- 1 tbsp Vanilla Extract
- Juice of 1 Lime
- 2 tbsp Coconut Sugar(optional)
- Ice cubes (optional, for a colder smoothie)

Serving Size: 2

Instructions:

1. Start by removing the peel and seeds from the papaya and freezing until solid. If you're in a pinch for time, use papaya at room temperature and add ice.
2. In a blender, combine the ingredients
3. Blend all the ingredients together until you achieve a smooth and creamy consistency.
4. Once you're satisfied with the taste and texture, pour the smoothie into a glass and enjoy!

> **TIP** *Freeze sliced papaya in advance for an extra creamy texture after blending.*

ZABOKA TOAST

Haitians are well acquainted with "pen ak zaboka," or as others call it, avocado toast. These two ingredients are simple yet incredibly delicious. Over the years, I've observed the surge in popularity of avocado toast, appearing on nearly every restaurant's breakfast menu as the go-to veggie option. It's so easy that not enjoying it at home almost feels like a crime!

Let's talk bread – I've discovered that sourdough is the best gut-healthy option among the numerous bread types available worldwide, and it pairs exceptionally well with avocado. While Haitians craft delightful warm bread, my digestive system can only handle so much gluten in a week. Thus, I deeply appreciate the qualities of sourdough and its beneficial bacteria. For someone who craves variety in meals, I understand that simple avocado toast can become monotonous. For this reason, I've curated five versions of avocado toast for your enjoyment.

ZABOKA TOAST

The best breakfast, lunch and dinner option! Simply swap out your toppings to switch it's purpose.

Serving Time: 7-10min

Serving Size: 1

Ingredients:

- 1 Thick slice of Sourdough Bread
- ½ tsp Red Crushed Pepper
- ½ Avocado
- ½ tsp Salt
- ½ tsp Black Pepper
- 1 tbsp Bussin Butter (Substitute: Salted butter or grapeseed oil)

Instructions:

1. Begin by preheating a griddle or frying pan over medium-high heat.
2. Spread Bussin Butter (or your preferred substitute) on each side of the sourdough slice.
3. Toast each side of the slice until it turns a delightful golden brown.
4. Remove from heat and use a fork to add the avocado onto the slice. Mash the avocado until it becomes smooth.
5. Top it off with a sprinkle of salt, black pepper, and red crushed pepper. Enjoy it as it is or get creative by adding extra toppings!

TIP *To prolong your loaf of sourdough's freshness, freeze half of your loaf to prevent rapid spoilage.*

TOPPING COMBOS

Alternate topping combinations to spice up your Zaboka Toast - theres a pairing for every mood you may be in!

The Island Babe:

- 3 slices of Fried Sweet Plantain
- 1/2 Avocado
- Tbsp of Pink Pikliz
- Sprinkle of Scallion

The Earthy Babe:

- ½ of a Sliced Beet
- ½ Avocado
- Pickled Red Onions
- Handful Mixed Greens
- Drizzle of Honey
- Drizzle of Olive Oil

The Italian Babe:

- Handful of Arugula
- 1½ Avocado
- Drizzle of Olive Oil
- Juice of ½ Lemon
- Sprinkle of Parmesan Cheese

The Medi:

- 1 spoon of Hummus
- Cucumber Slices
- Sprinkle of Everything But the Bagel Seasoning

CHAPTER III

PLANTAIN SUPREMACY

PLANTAIN SUPREMACY

Let it be known: If you have a plantain at your disposal, you'll always have a meal.

Plantains are cherished fruits across the diaspora, but they hold a special place in my kitchen. You can fry, boil, steam, sauté, bake, and mash a plantain—each method yields a different, delightful meal with just a few added ingredients. Plantains truly reign supreme in the fruit kingdom. Few other fruits offer the versatility of being enjoyed both sweet and savory like a plantain. In Haitian cuisine, we typically use green plantains in our recipes, so there's seldom time for them to ripen. I want you to know how to elevate a plantain beyond the typical frying method. I've crafted three delectable ways for you to savor plantains, whether ripe or not.

PLANTAIN-ADAS

When I first launched The Haitian Croissant in 2020, this recipe went viral. Believe it or not, I began making Plantain-adas in 2017, and I hadn't come across a recipe for them prior. I like to believe that I pioneered this dish and will continue to do so. Crafting these hand pies requires a bit more time and love than most of my other dishes, but the effort is absolutely worthwhile. Upon my venture into plant-based dishes in 2017, I filled Plantain-adas with black beans, and they were undeniably delicious. Nowadays, when preparing these treats for others, I offer three filling options: shiitake mushroom, ground beef, or black beans. All three options are equally delectable and prepared with the same ingredients.

Serving Time: 40 min

Ingredients:

- 4 ripe yellow Plantains
- ½ cup All-Purpose Flour
- 8 Shiitake Mushrooms
- 1 medium-sized Carrot
- 1 medium sized Shallot
- 1/2 tsp Turmeric
- 3 cloves of Garlic
- 1.5 tbsp Curry Powder
- 1 tsp Onion Powder
- 1 tsp Salt
- 1 tsp Pepper
- ½ tbsp Scotch Bonnet Hot Sauce
- Avocado Oil for Frying
- Plastic Wrap
- 4.4" Circle Cookie Cutter or Small Bowl

Serving Size: 3-4

Instructions:

1. In a medium stockpot, bring 6 cups of water to a boil
2. Slice the ends off the plantains and place them into the boiling water until the plantains slightly protrude from their peel.
3. Once boiled, remove the plantains from their peel and transfer them to a large mixing bowl.
4. Add ¼ cup of AP flour to the plantains and mix with your hands until a dough is formed
5. Place the dough in the refrigerator for one hour until it cools.
6. Cut the mushrooms, carrot, shallot, and garlic into fine cubes.
7. In a medium frying pan over medium heat, add one tablespoon of avocado oil.
8. For 4-6min Pan-fry the mushrooms, carrot, and garlic until they become soft.

Instructions continued :

9. Season the mushroom mixture with curry powder, onion powder, salt, pepper, and Scotch Bonnet hot sauce. Adjust the hot sauce to your preferred level of spiciness.
10. Remove the mushroom mixture from heat and set it aside for 30 minutes to cool.
11. On a clean countertop, lay out a sheet of plastic wrap. Sprinkle AP flour onto the plastic wrap and roll out the plantain dough until it's approximately ¼" thick.
12. Spoon out 2 tablespoons of the mushroom filling about 1.5" away from the edge of the rolled-out dough.
13. Using the plastic wrap, flip the dough over to cover the mushroom filling, creating the shape of a hand pie.
14. Use the circle cookie cutter to create a half-circle shape, forming the plantain-ada hand pie shape.
15. Repeat the process until all of the plantain dough is used, yielding approximately 4-5 plantainadas. For a larger batch, boil four plantains.
16. In a medium frying pan, coat it with avocado oil. Shallow fry the plantainadas for 3 minutes on each side until they turn golden brown.
17. Remove them from the oil and place them on a plate with paper towels to remove any excess oil.
18. Serve the Plantain-adas hot with your choice of hot sauce. Enjoy your flavorful Plantain-adas!

TIP: *Plastic wrap will be your best friend when forming these Plantain-adas, after forming your first two, it gets easier!*

BANNANN BROWNS

Hashbrowns are my preferred way to enjoy potatoes, and one day, I decided to swap potatoes for plantains, and I haven't looked back since. This recipe is another one of my viral hits, and for good reason. Plantains possess a unique ability to achieve a remarkable level of crispiness, resulting in an explosion of flavors in your mouth! When paired with the avocado lime crema and the savory saltiness of the plantain, it's a culinary match made in heaven. I hope to see these delightful creations on breakfast menus worldwide one day.

Serving Time: 20-25 minutes **Serving Size: 2**

Ingredients:

- Large Bowl of Cold Water
- 1 Green Plantain with a few spots of yellow
- 1 tsp Garlic Powder
- 1 tsp Onion Powder
- ½ tbsp Cornstarch
- 1 tsp Paprika
- 1 tsp Salt
- Avocado Oil for Pan Frying
- Clean Cheesecloth or Kitchen Towel

Avocado Crema:
- 1/2 Avocado
- ¼ cup Coconut Creme
- 1tbsp Fresh Lime Juice
- 1/2 cup Fresh Cilantro
- ½ tsp Salt
- 1/2 tsp Black Pepper

Instructions:

1. Remove the peel from the plantain.
2. 2. In a medium bowl, use a cheese grater to grate the plantain.
3. Cover the grated plantain in water to rinse off the starch, then discard the water and repeat the rinsing process one more time.
4. Using a clean cheesecloth or kitchen towel, squeeze out any excess water from the shredded plantain, using your hands to ring out the water.
5. In a dry medium-sized mixing bowl, place the shredded plantain and season it with garlic powder, onion powder, cornstarch, paprika, and salt. Thoroughly mix until all ingredients are incorporated
6. In a medium frying pan, coat it with avocado oil.
7. Using a tablespoon, scoop out piles of the plantain mixture into the hot oil.
8. Fry the first side for 3-5 minutes until the edges look golden brown. Once the edges are golden brown, use a spatula to flip over each bannann brown. After flipping, press down onto each one with a spatula.
9. Once both sides are golden brown, remove them from the fryer and place them on a baking sheet or plate with paper towels to extract any extra oil.
10. Avocado Crema: In a blender, add all the crema ingredients and blend until completely smooth.
11. Serve the Bannann Browns with avocado crema on the side and enjoy!

TIP *Plantains that are green have more crunch, yellow will be soft and less crispy. A green plantain with spots of yellow are perfect for this dish.*

ROCK THE BOAT

Plantain boats are a Caribbean favorite, although not specifically a Haitian dish, I wish they were! As mentioned earlier, with just one plantain, you're always ready for a meal. I often find myself with one or two ripe plantains when I purchase a bunch, making this recipe ideal for those occasions. While my recipe calls for shiitake mushrooms, you can truly fill these with a wide array of ingredients, such as fried tofu, meat, seafood, or even beans and cheese. The kitchen is your canvas.

Serving Time: 15 min

Serving Size: 1

Ingredients:

- 1 Yellow & Bruised Plantain (Extra Ripe)
- ½ c Chopped Shiitake Mushrooms
- 2 tbsp Jerk Seasoning
- ½ tsp Cayenne Pepper
- ¼ of an Avocado
- Pink Pikliz Onions
- Sliced Scallions for garnish
- 2 tbsp avocado oil

Instructions:

1. 1. To start remove the peel from the ripe plantain and slice it down the center lengthwise, creating a hotdog bun shape.
2. Preheat 1 tablespoon of avocado oil in a small frying pan.
3. Pan fry each side of the plantain on medium-high heat for 4-6 minutes each until they turn brown.
4. . Remove the plantain from the frying pan and add in the remaining 1 tablespoon of avocado oil. Then, add the mushrooms, jerk seasoning, and cayenne pepper.
5. . Pan fry the mushrooms for 4-6 minutes until they are well coated and slightly crisp.
6. On a large plate, spread open the fried plantain and pour the mushroom mixture into the center. Top it with sliced avocado, Pink Pikliz Onions, and garnish with sliced scallions.
7. Enjoy your Rock the Boat

TIP *The riper the plantain, the better it works for this recipe. Feel free to swap out the mushroom for any form of protein!*

CHAPTER IV

FOR A CROWD

FOR A CROWD

Entertaining guests can be one of the best aspects of living on your own, provided you are well-prepared. Preparing an extensive spread can be quite daunting, especially for someone who is not accustomed to it. Instead of overwhelming yourself by attempting a grand culinary endeavor, start with one or two of the following recipes. You'll pleasantly surprise your guests, leaving them with satisfied bellies. Whenever I meet up with friends around the world, they unfailingly request my Beef Patés with Diri ak Pwa or the Loving Lasagna.

PATÉ KODÉ

Hand pies, known by various names throughout the African diaspora like paté, empanadas, or pastelillos, share a common trait – a flaky dough exterior enveloping a flavorful filling. In Haitian cuisine, we have both baked "paté" found in Haitian bakeries and a deep-fried version called "paté kodé," typically sold by street vendors. While I wasn't allowed to eat street food as a child, I decided to give paté kodé a try when I traveled to Haiti on my own, and it was delightful. Depending on who makes the dough, it can sometimes be quite dense. In my recipe, I prefer using premade discos available in Latinx stores (Goya discos are my favorite). Paté Kodé serves as a fantastic appetizer or a satisfying meal when paired with a salad. As a self-proclaimed culinary nomad, I have acquired friend groups in different parts of the world, and whenever I visit, they invariably request this specific recipe, every single time.

PATÉ KODÉ

Serving Time: 40 Minutes

Serving Size: 5

Ingredients:

- ½ pound Ground Turkey or Plant-Based Ground Meat
- 2 Cloves of Garlic (Minced)
- ½ yellow Onion, Finely chopped
- ½ tbsp All-Purpose Seasoning
- Salt & Pepper to taste
- 2 tbsp Epis
- 1 packet of Sazon
- ½ tbsp Red Crushed Pepper
- Avocado oil for frying
- 1 packet of defrosted Goya Empanada Discos for Frying

Instructions:

1. In a medium frying pan, place lean ground beef (or meat substitute) and cook over medium-high heat. After 2 minutes, add minced garlic, onion, all-purpose seasoning, epis, sazon, and red crushed pepper while the meat is cooking.
2. Once seasoned, mix and break up the ground meat, and cook thoroughly for 7-9 minutes.
3. After the meat is fully cooked, season with salt and pepper to taste, then remove from heat.
4. Take one pack of defrosted Goya Empanada discos and place about 1.5 tbsp of the meat mixture onto each disco.
5. Seal the edges by pressing with your hand and then double-seal the edges of the paté with a fork. Using a fork ensures that the meat will not spill out during the deep-frying process.
6. In a medium-sized saucepan, pour in avocado oil until it reaches about 2 inches from the bottom of the saucepan. Heat the oil until it's hot over medium-high heat. To test if the oil is ready for frying, place the end of a wooden spoon into the oil. If bubbles form around the wooden spoon, it's ready for frying!
7. Carefully place 2 patés into the hot oil at a time. Each side should take 1-2 minutes to become golden brown. Flip them once they are golden brown on one side. Once both sides are golden brown, remove them and place them on a baking rack or a plate lined with paper towels.

Always keep a pack of empanada discos in your freezer to quickly make, crowd-pleasing Paté Kodé for house guests!

THE PASTA DUMP

This Pasta Dump is my personal choice for a quick and delectable meal. It strikes a balance between classic spicy rigatoni and a vodka sauce. Instead of heavy cream, this recipe features canned coconut milk as a gut-friendly alternative. I affectionately call it my "Whatever is in the fridge" pasta because I enjoy folding in different leftover veggies or proteins I find in the fridge. Incorporating seasonal vegetables not only imparts a delightful flavor to this dish but also boosts its nutritional value.

Serving Time: 20-25min

Serving Size : 2-3

Ingredients:

- 2 tablespoons Tomato Paste
- ¼ Red Onion, diced
- 2 cloves of Garlic, minced
- ⅓ cup Canned Coconut Milk
- ½ tablespoon Red Crushed Pepper
- 2 servings of Rigatoni
- 2 tablespoons Salt
- Salt & Pepper to Taste
- 6 cups Water (for boiling pasta, set aside 1/4 to add to pasta sauce)
- 1 tablespoon Avocado oil
- 1 tablespoon Essential Epis

Optional add-ins: Shredded Zucchini, Seasoned Ground Meat, Spinach, Mushrooms, Beets

Instructions:

1. In a medium pot, boil water and add in pasta. Follow the pasta box directions to cook the pasta until al dente.
2. In a large saucepan, add avocado oil and tomato paste. Cook it down until the tomato paste turns two shades darker, approximately after 3 minutes.
3. Add in red crushed pepper, garlic, red onion, and Essential Epis. Stir until thoroughly blended. After 3 minutes, pour in canned coconut milk and add ¼ cup of Pasta water to the mixture.
4. Once thoroughly blended, add in the pasta and turn off the heat. Stir in mixins such as spinach and mushrooms.
5. Serve hot with a side of delicious sourdough bread and enjoy!

TIP *I love mezze rigatoni, but swap out rigatoni for your favorite shape of pasta as you please!*

DIRI AK PWA

Diri ak Pwa is Haitian Kreyol for rice and beans. While there are over five variations of Haitian rice and beans, there is only one considered our "Diri Nasyonal" (National rice), featuring red kidney beans. When properly prepared, it's practically a meal on its own. I enjoy topping my Diri ak Pwa with pink pikliz and some delectable Haitian sauce.

Serving Time: 40-45min

Ingredients:

- 2 tablespoons Essential Epis
- 4 Minced Garlic Cloves
- ¼ Medium Red Onion (Diced)
- 1 ½ cups Red Kidney Beans
- 4 Cloves
- 6 cups of water (will reduce down to 4 1/3 cups)
- 2 ½ cups Carolina gold Parboiled long-grain rice
- 1 teaspoon salt
- 1 tablespoon seasoning salt
- 1 Habanero Pepper
- 4 Sprigs of Thyme
- 1/3 cup Olive Oil

Serving Size: 4-5

Instructions:

1. In a medium-sized pot with a lid, boil 6 cups of water and kidney beans on medium heat for 45-55 minutes until kidney beans are medium soft to the touch. You should be able to squeeze them open with two fingers with a bit of force.
2. Strain the beans from the water and preserve 4 1/3 cups of the bean water and set it aside.
3. In the same pot, add olive oil. Once the oil is hot, add in red onion, minced garlic cloves, and Essential Epis. Sauté for 3 minutes.
4. Add in kidney beans and fry for 3 minutes, then cover the pot with a lid to fry beans for an additional 7 minutes. After 7 minutes, the beans should be soft with a few bursting open.
5. At this stage, add in 3 1/3 cups of bean water, seasoning salt, cloves, pepper, thyme, and salt to the pot.
6. In a medium mixing bowl, add in rice and rinse and strain it twice to wash off additional starch.
7. Once thoroughly strained, add rice to the bean water and let the rice come to a boil, which should take between 7-10 minutes.
8. As the water is boiling, add in the last cup of bean water to the pot and let the rice cook until most of the water has been absorbed by the rice. Once the majority of the water has been absorbed and the rice is visible through the water, cover the pot with the lid for 7-10 minutes on low heat.
9. Remove the lid, and the rice will have fully absorbed the water. With a fork, fluff the rice and let it sit for 5 minutes with the heat and lid off.
10. Remove the sprigs of thyme and the pepper.
11. Serve hot and fresh. Enjoy your Diri ak Pwa!

TIP *Pre-boil and freeze a cup of red kidney beans to have on hand for quick Diri ak Pwa preparation on the go.*

NOT SO BASIC RICE

Rice can be challenging for many cooks, especially newcomers. When preparing rice, be patient and kind to yourself, whether it's your first or hundredth attempt. Haitian white rice incorporates a few extra ingredients compared to a basic white rice recipe, and these additions are what make it so addictive! Haitians and rice are inseparable. Follow these steps, and you'll have delicious white rice that can be enjoyed on its own or with a delectable sauce.

Serving Time: 20-25min

Serving Size: 2

Ingredients:

- 1 cup Jasmine Rice
- 2 cups Water
- 1 tablespoon Salt
- 2 tablespoons Olive Oil
- 2 cloves
- 1 Scallion

Instructions:

1. In a medium bowl, wash and rinse the rice twice, until the rinsed water is mostly clear.
2. In a medium saucepot, add 2 tablespoons of olive oil and fry 1 scallion branch for 2 minutes.
3. Add the strained rice and water, salt, and cloves. Stir to combine.
4. On medium heat, allow the water to come to a boil and cook for 7-10 minutes until the rice absorbs the majority of the water.
5. Turn down the heat to low and cover with a lid for the rice to finish cooking. After 6-8 minutes, remove the lid and fluff the rice with a fork.
6. Taste-test the rice. If the rice is undercooked, add in a splash of water and cover with a lid to allow the rice to steam for 5 more minutes.
7. Serve hot and enjoy alone or with your choice of sauce, curry, or stew.

> **TIP:** With rice, always remember the 2:1 ratio, 2 cups water for every cup of rice, it will likely turn out perfectly most of the time with washed rice!

LOVING LASAGNA

My Loving Lasagna is a twist on my Godmother's recipe and is always a hit with a crowd. The key is the meat-to-cheese filling ratio: 2:1. I prefer more meat than cheese in my lasagna, so for every layer of cheese filling, there are two meat layers. For those who are lactose intolerant, this ratio is crucial. You can also opt for dairy-free alternatives and mushrooms in place of meat, both of which result in equally delicious outcomes.

Serving Time: 50-55min

Serving Size: 4-5

Ingredients:

- 8 lasagna noodles
- 2 cups tomato sauce
- 2 tablespoons brown sugar
- 2 teaspoons dried basil
- 1/2 teaspoon red crushed pepper (adjust to taste for spiciness)
- 1/4 teaspoon cayenne pepper (adjust to taste for spiciness)
- Salt and pepper to taste
- 2 garlic cloves, minced
- 1/2 red onion, finely chopped
- 1/2 teaspoon garlic powder
- - 1 1/2 cups mozzarella cheese, shredded
- 1 cup ricotta cheese
- 1/2 cup Parmesan cheese, grated
- 1/2 pound ground beef or plant-based ground
- 2 tablespoons avocado oil
- 9x13 inch baking pan

Instructions:

1. Preheat your oven to 375°F (190°C).
2. Cook the lasagna noodles according to the package instructions until they are al dente. Drain, rinse with cold water, and set aside.
3. In a large skillet, heat the avocado oil over medium-high heat. Add the chopped red onion and minced garlic, and sauté for about 2-3 minutes until they become fragrant and translucent.
4. Add the ground beef or plant-based ground to the skillet. Cook, breaking it apart with a spoon, until it's browned and cooked through. Drain any excess fat if needed.
5. Stir in the tomato sauce, brown sugar, dried basil, red crushed pepper, cayenne pepper, garlic powder, salt, and pepper. Let the sauce simmer for 5-7 minutes, allowing the flavors to meld together. Adjust seasoning to taste.
6. In a separate bowl, combine the ricotta cheese and half of the Parmesan cheese. Mix well.

Instructions continued:

7. To assemble the lasagna, spread a thin layer of the meat sauce in the bottom of the 9x13-inch baking pan.
8. Place 4 lasagna noodles on top of the sauce, slightly overlapping to cover the bottom of the pan.
9. Spread ¾ of the ricotta cheese mixture over the noodles.
10. Sprinkle half of the mozzarella cheese over the ricotta layer.
11. Add another thick layer of meat sauce on top of the cheese.
12. Place the remaining 4 lasagna noodles over the sauce.
13. Repeat with the remaining ricotta cheese mixture, mozzarella cheese, and meat sauce.
14. Sprinkle the remaining Parmesan cheese over the top.
15. Cover the baking pan with aluminum foil and bake in the preheated oven for 25-30 minutes.
16. Remove the foil and bake for an additional 10-15 minutes, or until the lasagna is bubbly and the cheese on top is golden brown.
17. Allow the lasagna to cool for a few minutes before serving. Slice and serve hot!

TIP: *The brown sugar adds an extra kick to the tomato sauce, so don't skip it!*

TI PASSION COCKTAIL

It's no secret that passion fruit is my favorite fruit. It's versatile yet delightful as a simple juice. There was a time when I always kept a bottle of passion fruit juice in my fridge, but these days I savor it as an occasional treat. A few basic ingredients combined with passion fruit create an exquisite cocktail or mocktail. As a home cook and entertainer, it's valuable to know how to make a variety of cocktails. If you only learn one, let it be this one!

Serving Time: 7min   **Serving Size: 1**

Ingredients:

- 0.75 oz Lime Juice
- 1.5 oz Rhum Barbancourt
- 1/4 Can of Old Jamaica Ginger Beer (87.5 ml)
- 87.5 ml Passion Fruit Juice
- 1 tsp Agave
- Handful of Ice

Instructions:

1. In a cocktail shaker, add ice, lime juice, Rhum Barbancourt, agave, and passion fruit juice.
2. Shake for 1 minute.
3. Pour into a whiskey glass over ice, then top with ginger beer.
4. Enjoy!

TIP: *This cocktail tastes just as delicious as a mocktail! Omit the rum as you please.*

CHAPTER VI
FOR THE SOUL

FOR THE SOUL

The sobering reality of moving out, whether you're venturing into independent living or sharing your space with a roommate, is that you're often distanced from your family, and that can be challenging. Whether you sense the onset of a cold or simply yearn for some comforting warmth, you might not have a family member close by to provide you with the care you're accustomed to receiving. Back in my childhood home, I was truly pampered, especially when illness struck. I vividly recall my first bout of sickness while living alone, and it was a jarring experience for me. My mother ended up driving for hours just to be with me (she's truly one of a kind). Over time, I came to realize that recipes from home possess the remarkable ability to make you feel as if you're right back there. What fantastic news it is to understand that you can employ food to forge a connection to your roots and discover solace in the nurturing embrace of culinary joy.

WARM HUG TEA

I hail from a lineage of healing women, particularly those who practiced herbalism. Whenever I fell ill as a child, my grandmother always had a herbal concoction for me to sip as soothing tea to ease my discomfort and aches. This recipe is an homage to my grandmother's remedy for warding off colds and the flu. This tea truly warms the soul, and after sipping a few mugs consistently, you should feel any seasonal virus making its exit from your system.

Serving Time: 25 min

Serving Size: 4

Ingredients:

- **3 cups Water**
- **2 Lemons, sliced**
- **2 Limes, sliced**
- **4 inches of grated Ginger**
- **2 tbsp Turmeric**
- **3 Cloves**
- **2 tbsp Honey**

Optional additional add-ins:
For anxiety- Holy Basil
For stomach pain-Garlic peel
For a cold- Paprika

Instructions:

1. In a medium saucepot, add water.
2. Add in lemons, limes, grated ginger, turmeric, cloves, and honey.
3. Simmer for 20 minutes.
4. Strain to serve and enjoy!

I keep ginger root on hand at all times; it's a lifesaver!

LIFE OF THE PARTY DONUTS

At the end of a meal, I always crave a little something sweet. Growing up, my Godmother Tandan would make delicious pineapple upside down cakes and I would immediately eat the pineapples and cherries off of the top- those two fruits smothered in sticky brown sugar are truly chefs kiss. To ensure with every bite you get a taste of that goodness, I created this donut recipe- that way there is no fight for the pineapple, everyone can enjoy it. These donuts are a bit of nostalgia in every bite and they never disappoint as a delightful nightcap.

Serving Time: 40 min

Seriving Size: 3 (makes 6 donuts)

Ingredients:

- 1 cup all-purpose flour
- 1/4 cup granulated sugar
- 1 teaspoon baking powder
- ¼ teaspoon salt
- ½ teaspoon ground cinnamon
- ¼ teaspoon nutmeg
- ½ cup + 1 tablespoon coconut milk
- 1 tablespoon pineapple juice
- 1 tablespoon applesauce
- 1 tablespoon melted vegan butter
- 1 teaspoon pure vanilla extract
- Zest of one lime

For the Topping:

- 3 canned pineapple rings
- Maraschino cherries
- ½ cup brown sugar as a substitute
- 1 tablespoon vegan butter for greasing

Instructions:

1. Preheat your oven to 350°F (175°C). Grease a standard donut pan with 1 tablespoon of vegan butter.
2. Prepare the Topping: Place the pineapple rings on a paper towel to remove excess moisture. In each donut cavity, sprinkle a little coconut sugar or brown sugar. Place a maraschino cherry in the center of each pineapple ring.
3. In a mixing bowl, whisk together the all-purpose flour, granulated sugar, baking powder, salt, ground cinnamon, and nutmeg.
4. In another bowl, mix together the coconut milk, pineapple juice, applesauce, melted vegan butter, vanilla extract, and lime zest.
5. Pour the wet ingredients into the dry ingredients and stir until just combined. Be careful not to overmix; a few lumps are okay.
6. Carefully spoon the batter into the donut pan cavities, making sure not to disturb the pineapple and cherry topping.
7. Bake in the preheated oven for 15-18 minutes or until the donuts are lightly golden and a toothpick inserted into the center comes out clean.
8. Allow the donuts to cool in the pan for a few minutes, then run a knife around the edges of each donut to loosen them. Place a wire rack on top of the pan and invert it to release the donuts. They should come out easily.
9. Serve the Pineapple Upside-Down Donuts with the pineapple and cherry topping facing upward.

TIP: *When feeling adventurous, enjoy with a scoop of fresh rhum raisin icecream, and a drizzle of Rhum Barbancourt for the full Haitian experience!*

YOU CAN COOK

Haitian Fusion cooking is characterized by its nuanced, and unique approach. The techniques inherent in Haitian cuisine laid the foundation for my cooking journey, allowing me to seamlessly integrate methods from various cuisines I've encountered worldwide. Through these recipes, my aspiration is for you to appreciate and incorporate the dual nature of Haitian flavors and techniques in your daily culinary experiences. I encourage you to proudly share with the world the newfound confidence that "I Can Cook."

THE HAITIAN CROISSANT FOUNDATION

Home is where the heart is, The Haitian Croissant Foundation was founded in 2021 after a year establishing The Haitian Croissant brand to share the wellness, agricultural and arts values held dearly by Ayida Solé. The foundation's mission is to empower Haitian youth with the tools and knowledge to be self-sustainable members of Haiti through agriculture, arts, and wellness education. The foundation strives to improve overall social, economic, and agricultural conditions in Haiti, with a focus on the improvement of those conditions for the community in Ferrier, Haiti.

To get involved:
@thehaitiancroissantfoundation
thehaitiancroissantfoundation@gmail.com
www.thehaitiancroissantfoundation

Photography:
Photos on pages: 4, 18, 23,24, 29,38,41,42,55,65, 69, 72-73, 76 by Brittany Belo

Photos on pages: 26, 30,32,35, 36, 44-45, 48-49, 56-57, 70,81, 85, 88,89 by Myesha Evon

Photos on pages: 10, 13, 14, 16-17, 47,59, 60,78,87 by Jean Oscar A
Photos on pages: 53, 66-67 by Ayida Solé
All photography edits: Myesha Evon

Creative Copyright: Amariah L. DeJesus
Creative Editor: Julie Ann Elliston
Photo Creative Assistant: Saunders Ervin

Cover:
Art Director: Ayida Solé
Illustration of Woman: Syrine Ben Slimane
Assitant Art Director: Noahamin Taye